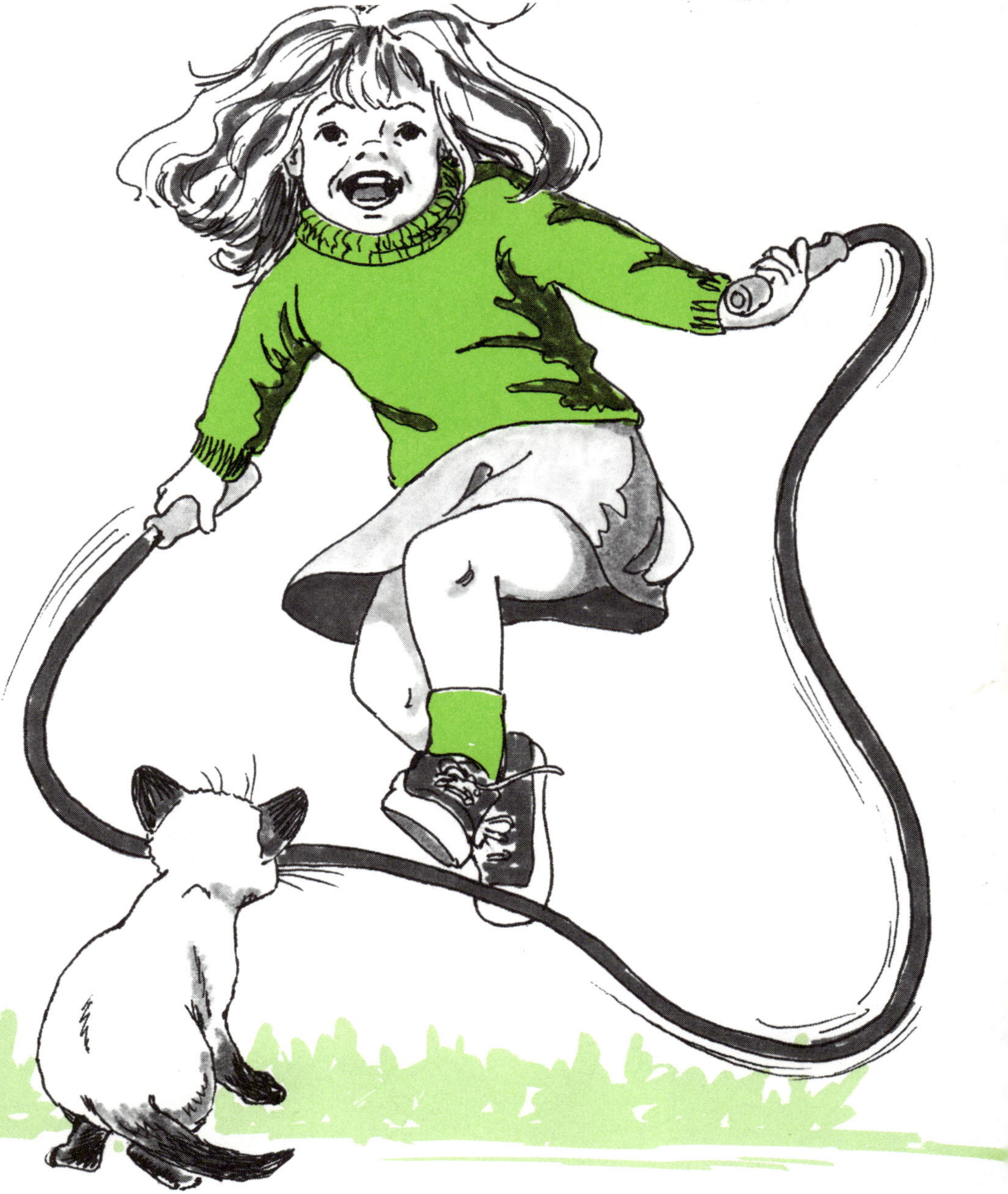

"Hi!

Do you have a minute, or two, or maybe three, so we can talk together?"

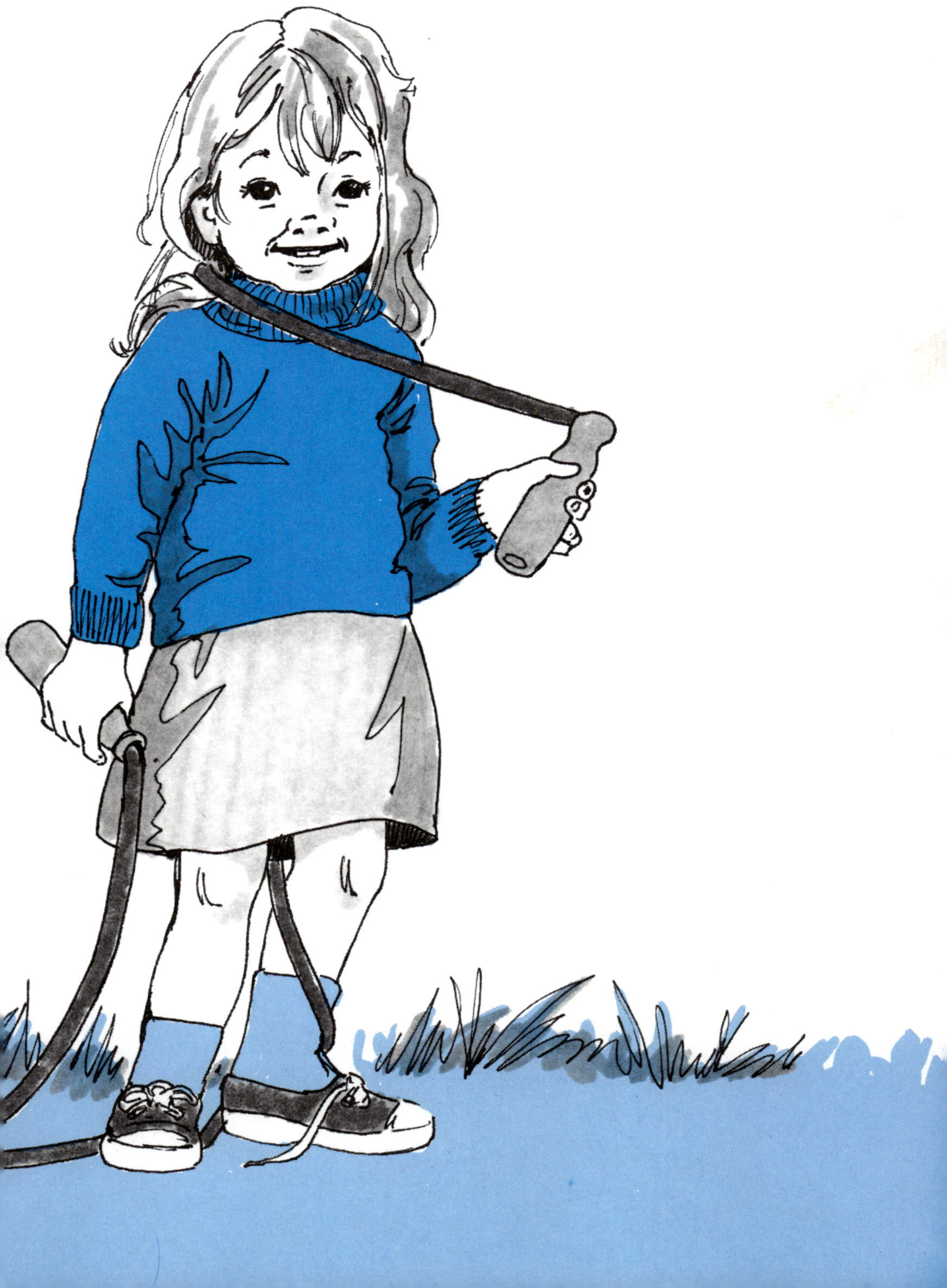

"I want to tell you about my Friend, my very best Friend.
But,

I can't even tell you if my Friend is old, or young. And I have never seen the color of His eyes.

I don't even know if my Friend is short, or tall.

But,

there is one thing that I do know about Him. He is not an animal like a rabbit, or a frog.

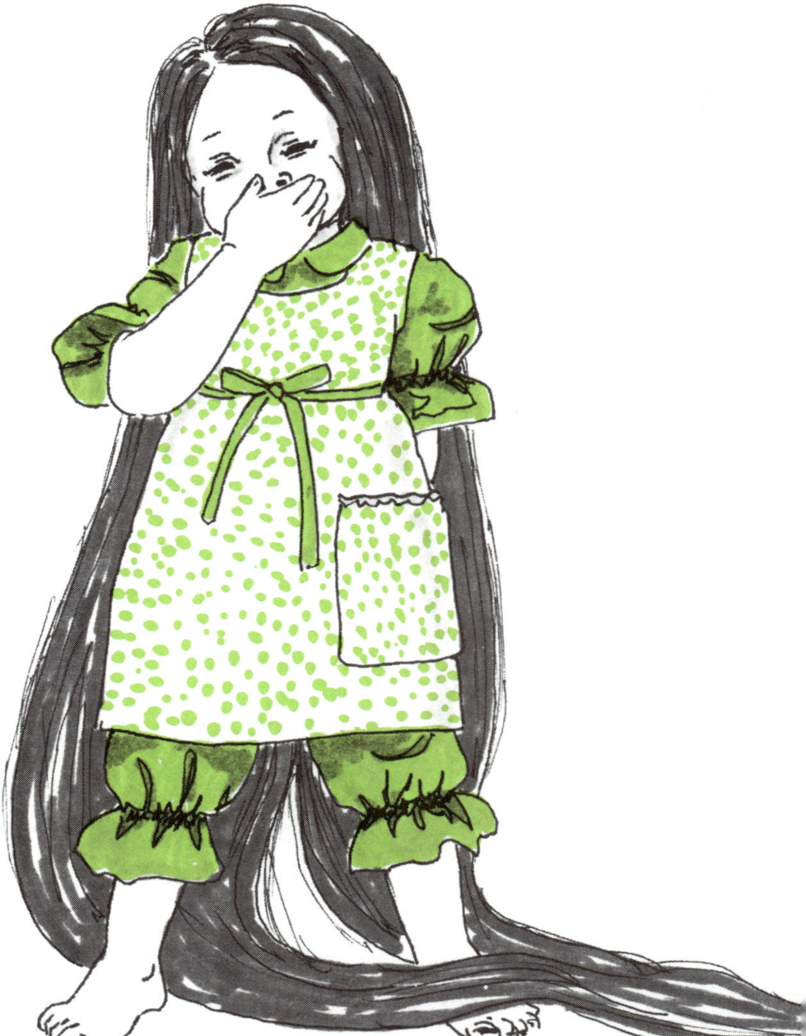

His hair might be long, or it could be short, and I don't even know what color it is. But I don't care, because He is still my very best Friend.

Whenever I go outdoors to play, I know that my Friend was there first, because He leaves flowers for me to smell and to look at.

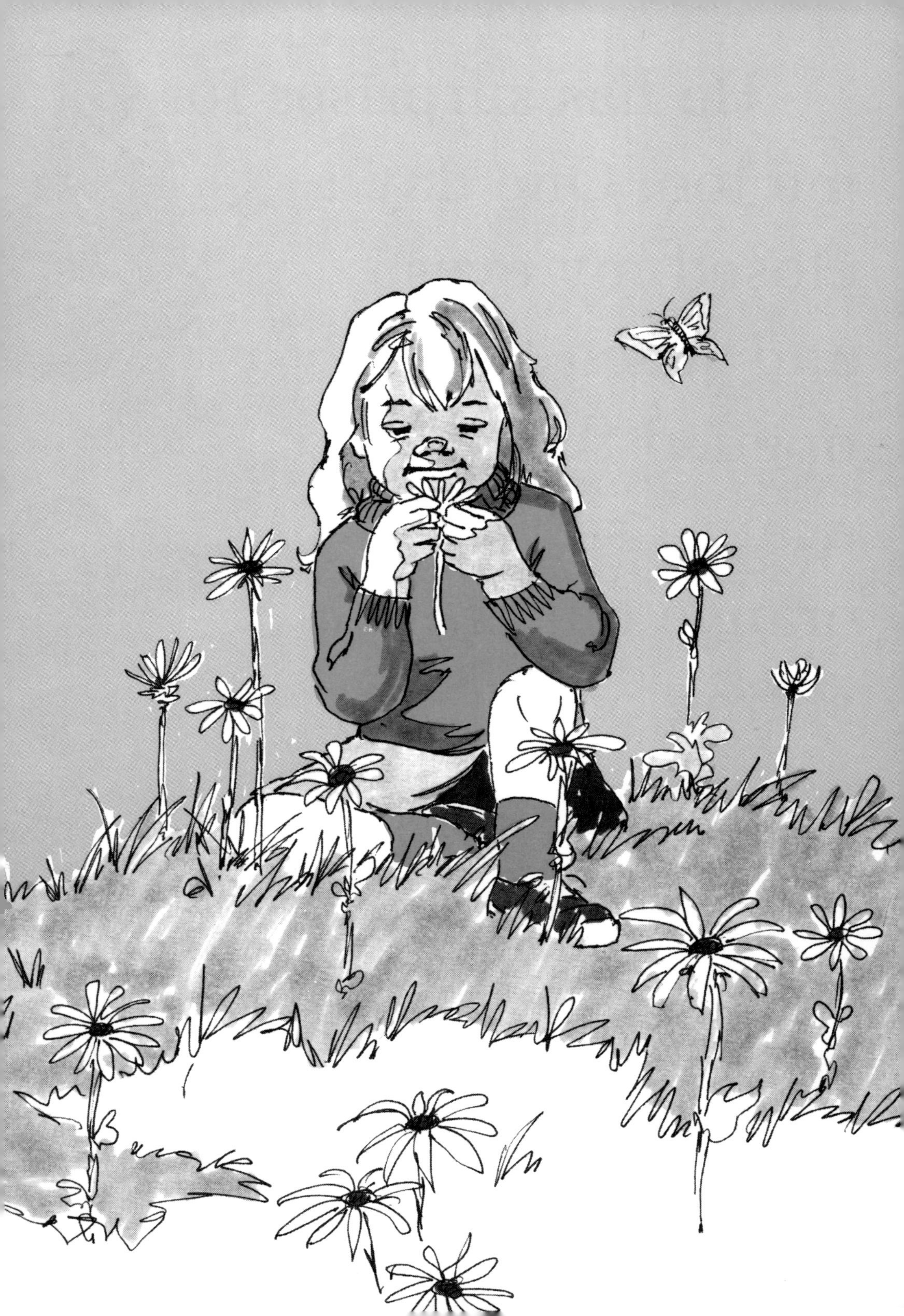

He has surprises for me too. One day I closed my eyes, and when I opened them again I saw an orange butterfly sitting on a flower.

At another time,

a bird sang to me.

Everyone that has ever lived was once a boy, or a girl, even my Friend. He likes all boys and girls.

OH, YES, My Friend's name is, JESUS!

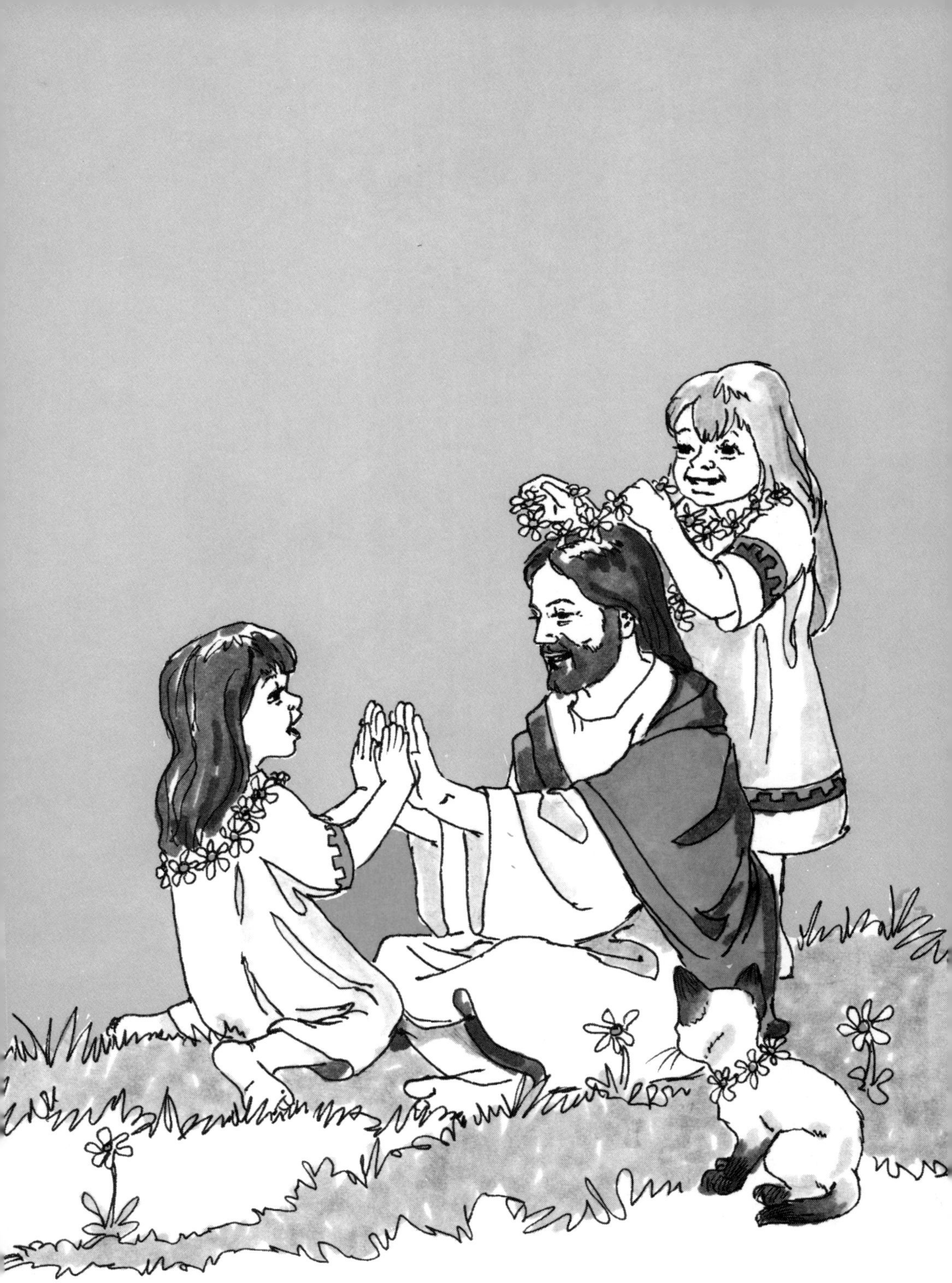

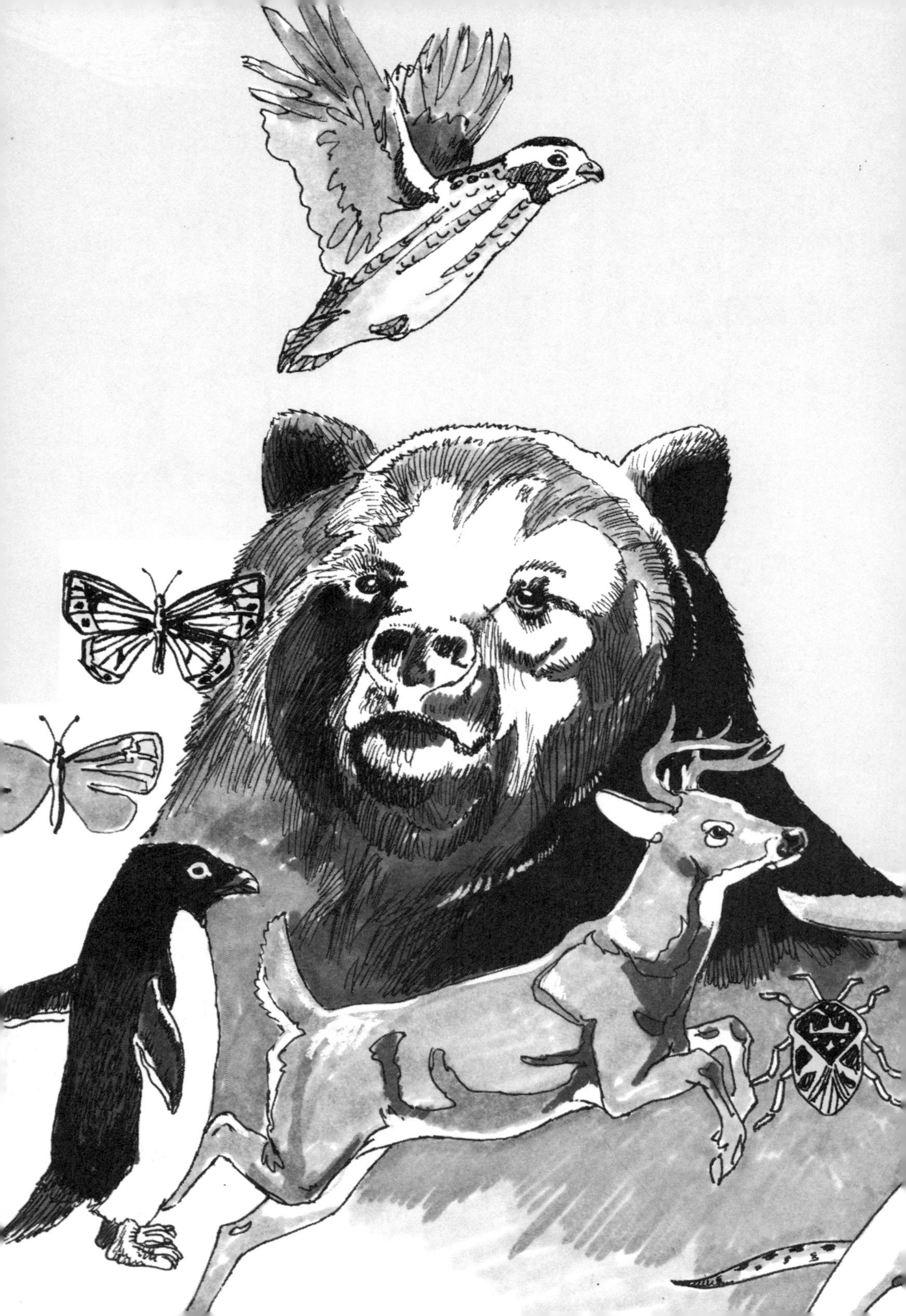

Grown-up people call Him God. They worship Him, and they teach me how to obey Him.

They say that my Friend made the world and everything in it, even me.

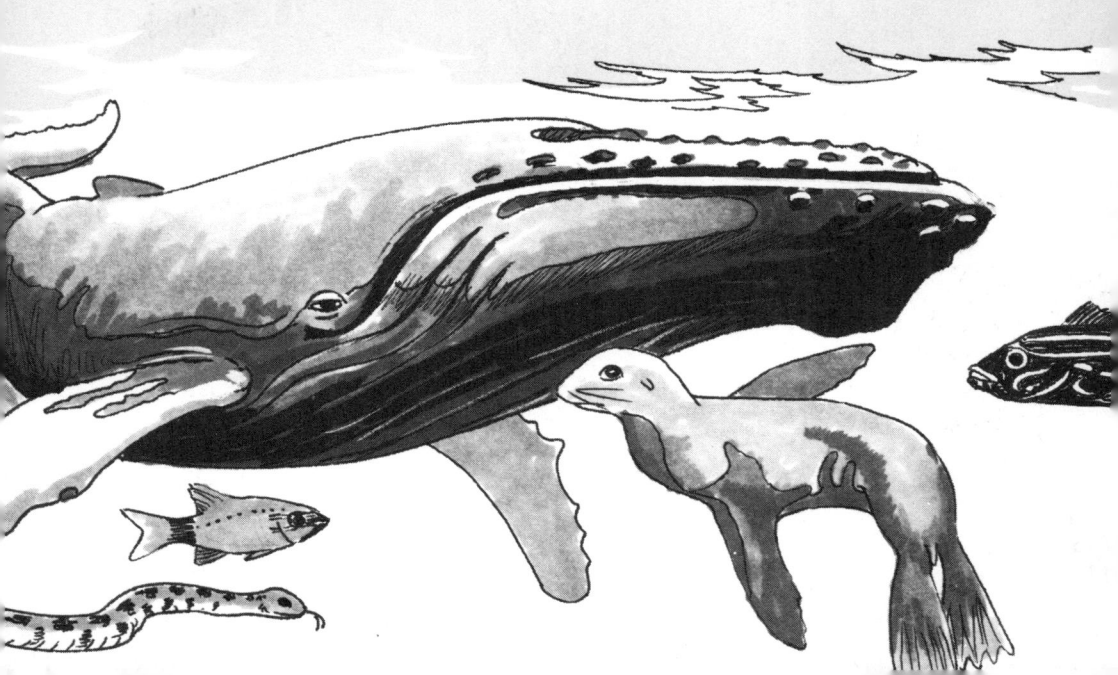

Well, He can be God if He wants to, but I like Him better as my best Friend.

Because, as friends,

we can talk together in secret, and I can tell Him everything I do.

He makes me laugh sometimes with the things He made, like "Sleepy" my cat, who plays with her tail.

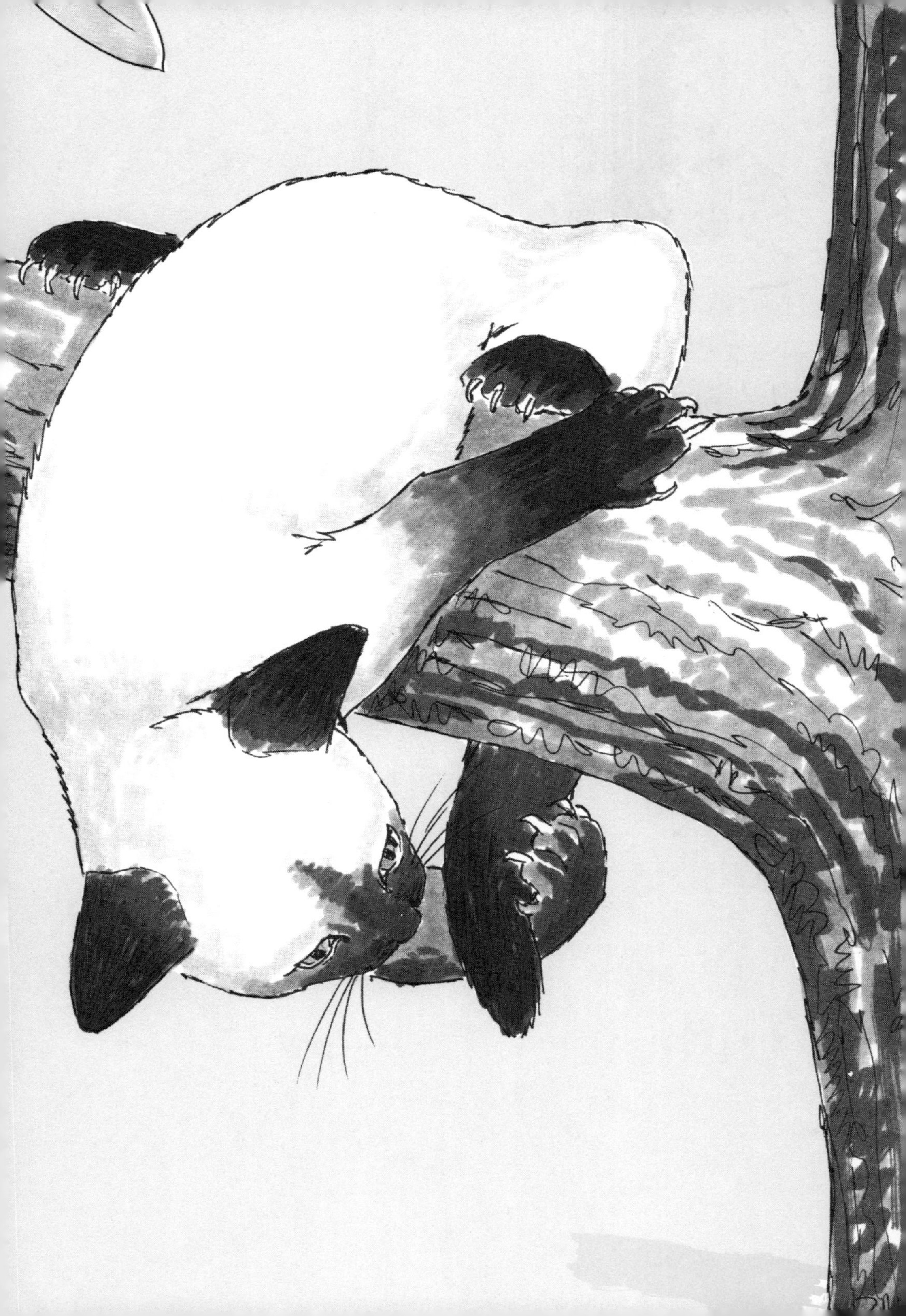

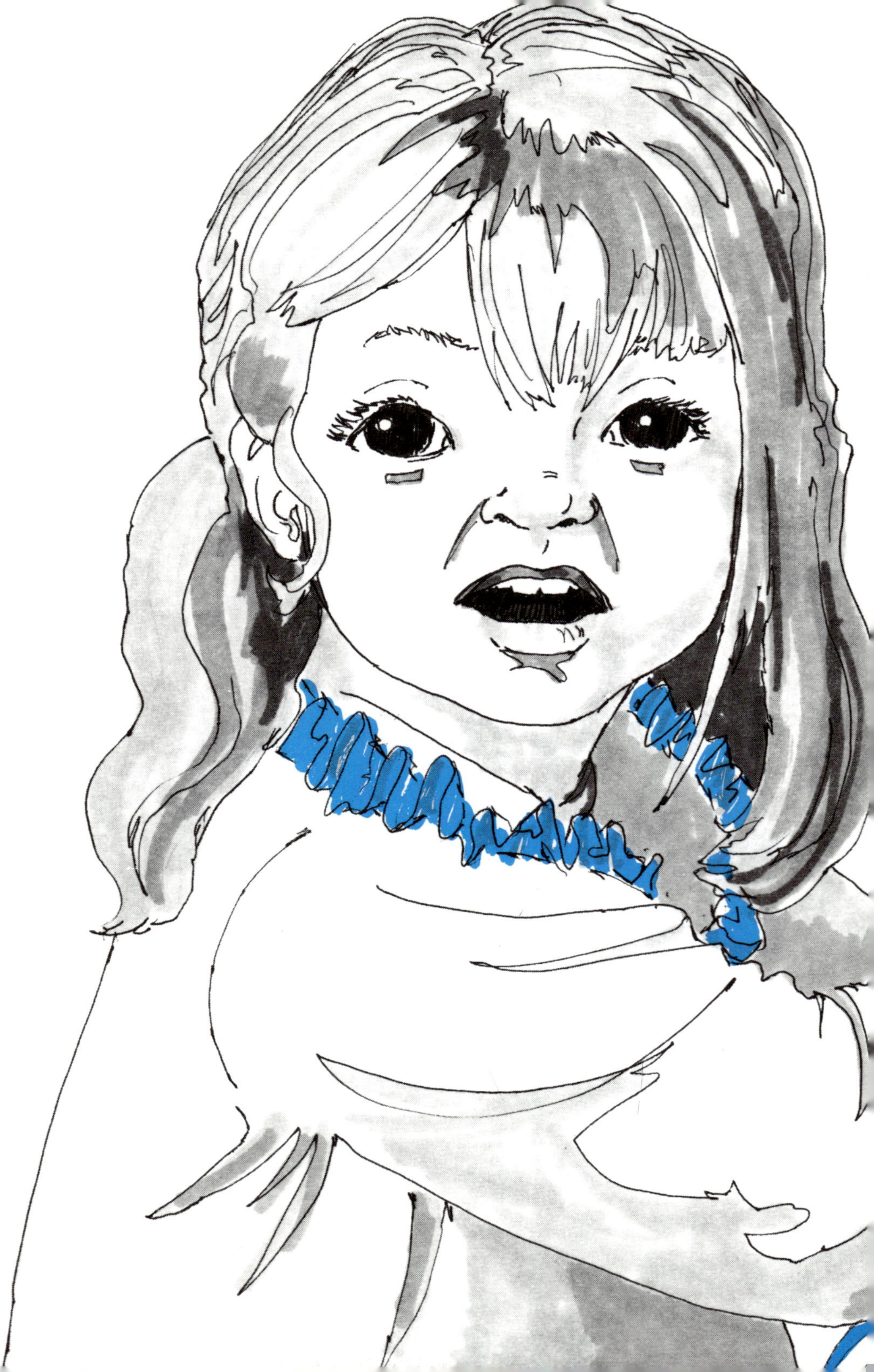

We have lots of fun, my best Friend and I. But here is a secret just between you and me.

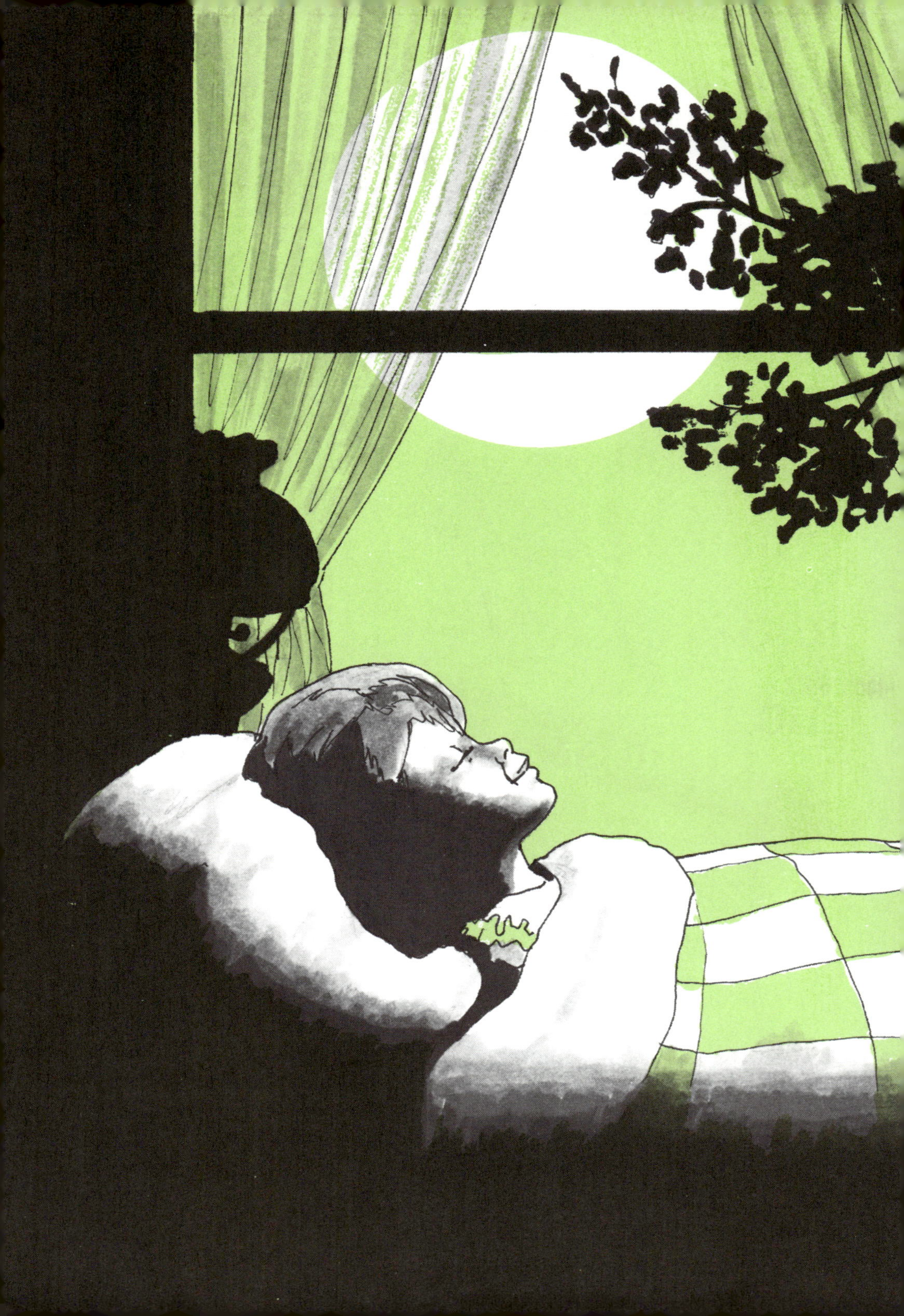

The time I like my Friend JESUS the best, is when I get sleepy and tired at night. Because when my eyes are almost closed,

my mommy or my daddy tiptoes into my room and quietly kisses me good night.
 It's then that I smile to myself in the dark, and I feel good all
 over.

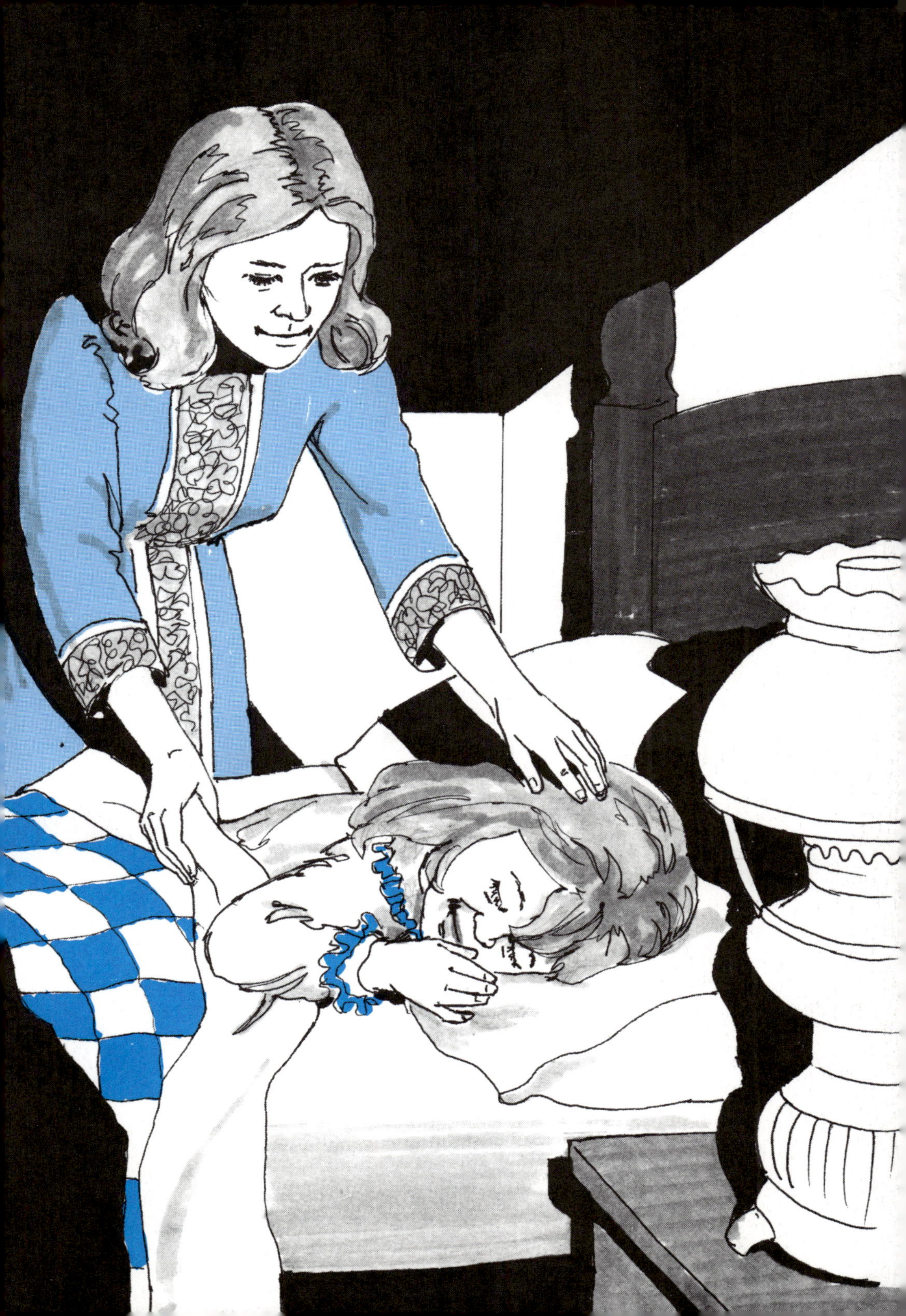

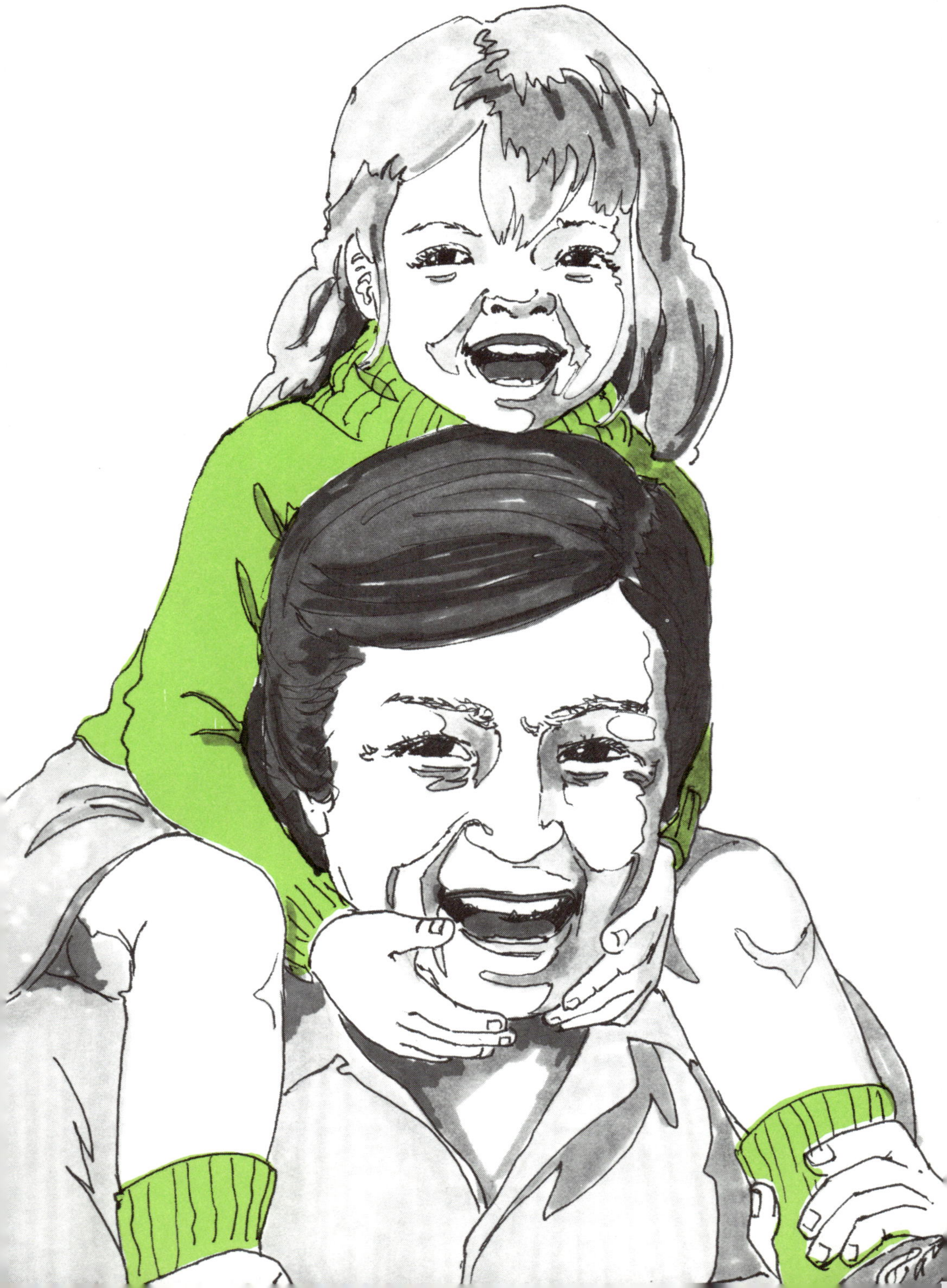

And sometimes I whisper, if I'm not asleep, to my best Friend JESUS, and I say, "Thank You for giving my mommy and my daddy to me, and for putting your love way down deep inside them."

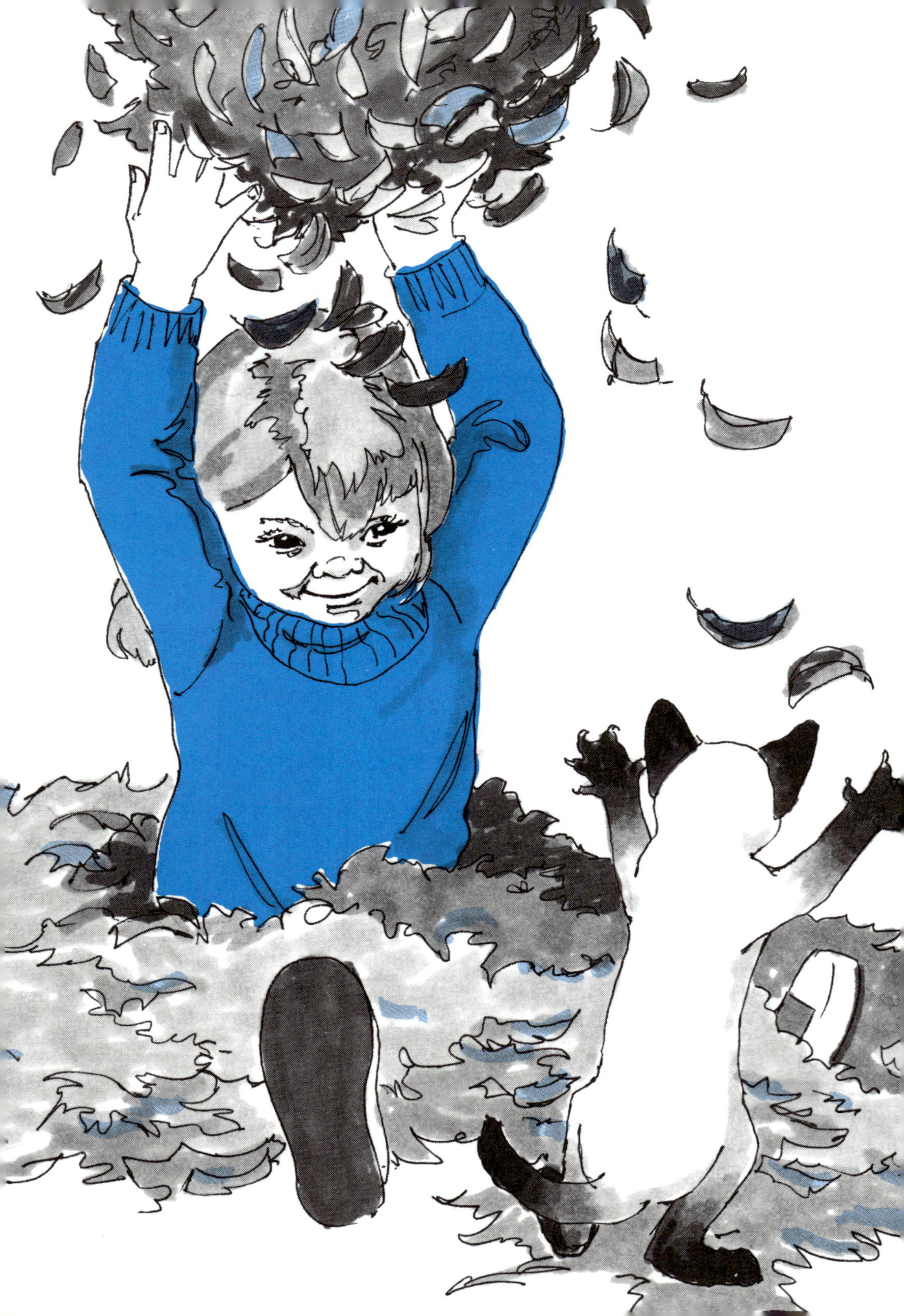

I love my Friend
JESUS, and I want you
to love Him too. He
made us a pretty world
to live in and filled it
full of good things
to have fun with.

And we should thank
Him for all of it.

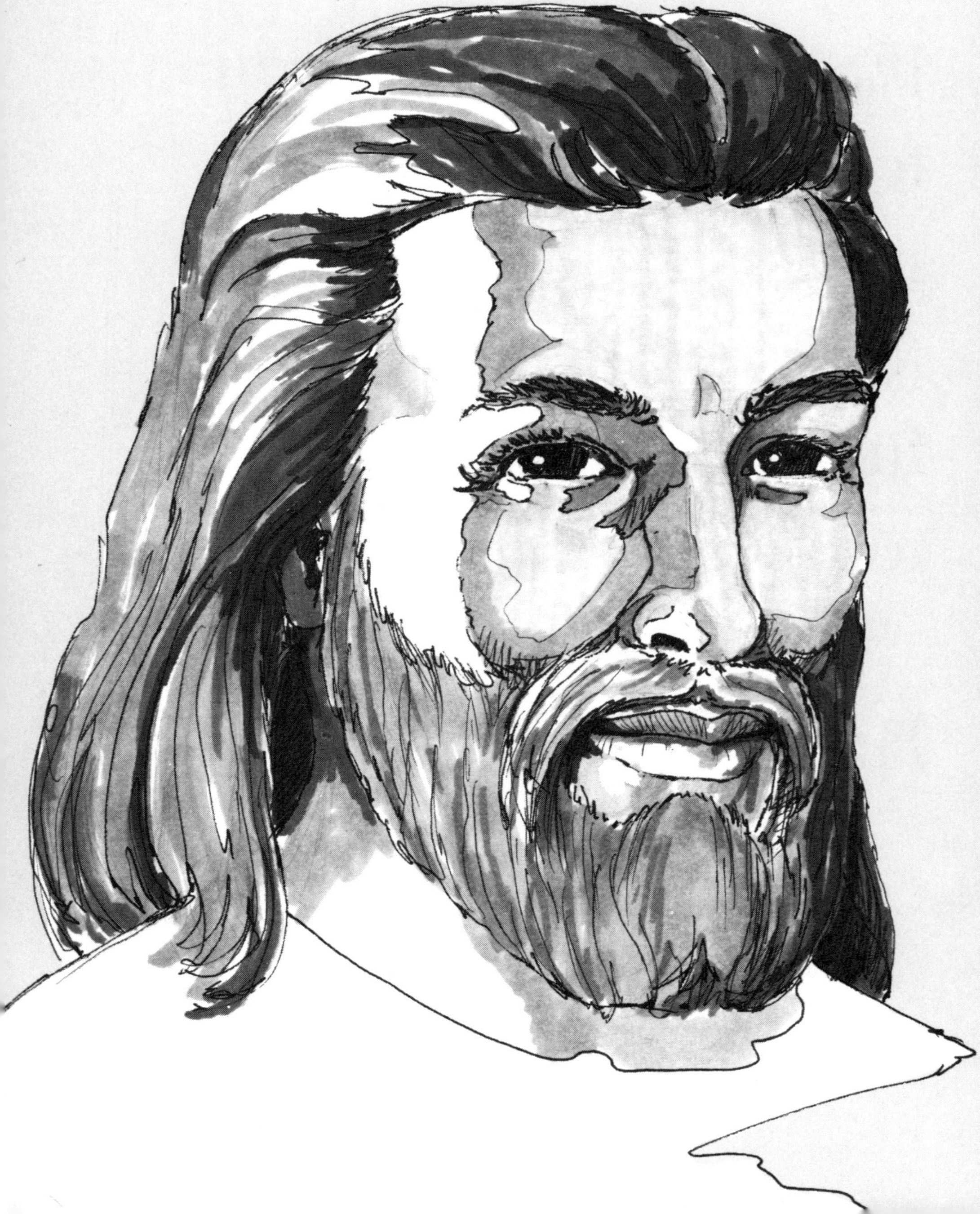